WHO
BROUGHT THE BREAD?

A Bible Mystery

The Scripture setting for this story can be found
in Matthew 14:13-21, Mark 6:30-44, Luke 9:10-1,
and John 6:1-14.

The Standard Publishing Company, Cincinnati, Ohio
A division of Standex International Corporation
Text © 1994 by Bob Hartman
Illustrations © 1994 by The Standard Publishing Company
All rights reserved. Printed in the United States of America
Library of Congress Catalog Card Number 94-10176
01 00 99 98 97 96 95 94   5 4 3 2 1
ISBN 0-7847-0188-8
Cataloging-in-Publication data available
Designed by Coleen Davis

WHO
BROUGHT THE BREAD?

A Bible Mystery

by Bob Hartman
illustrated by Terri Steiger

STANDARD
PUBLISHING
Cincinnati, Ohio

Huldah's chores were done for the day.
The washing, the sewing, the cleaning up.

And now she was determined to go to the hillside
and see what all this fuss was about.

"Jesus this. Jesus that." It was all she'd heard for days.
Now she would see for herself.

Huldah huffed and hurried
her way up the hill.
It was getting late,
and the higher she climbed,
the lower the sun dropped
behind her,
dropped its orange light
into the lake,
and stretched her wide shadow
thin and tall.

Then Huldah saw the crowd —
gathered in groups,
like bunches of grapes.
Then Huldah heard the crowd —
noisy and loud,
like a storm at sea.
Then Huldah sniffed and — OH!
What a smell she smelled!
The air was thick with the crusty
perfume of fresh-baked bread.

And from that moment she could think of nothing else.
Her head was filled with one question, and one question only —
Who brought the bread?

Huldah knew a thing or two about bread, you see.
For three years running, she had been voted "Bethsaida's Best Baker."
And bread — barley bread — was her specialty.

Picking the grain. Grinding it to flour.
Sorting the measures. Mixing in the water.
Kneading in the leaven. Leaving it to rise.

And then baking it with . . .
well, that was Huldah's secret.

"Huldah, over here!" called Joanna, Huldah's neighbor.
"Come join us," Joanna said.
"What are you doing?" asked Huldah.
"What does it look like we're doing?" laughed Joanna.
"We're eating. We're eating bread and fish."

"And may I say," added Joanna's sister, Susanna,
"that this is the best bread and fish I have ever tasted."
Huldah marched over to Joanna
and grabbed a chunk of bread out of her friend's hand.
"The best bread?" she huffed. "Impossible!"

Huldah broke
the bread in half.

She held it right under her nose
and breathed in deeply.

The more Huldah chewed, the more she worried. But she was determined not to let it show. "Hmm," she sniffed. "Barley bread. Not bad. Almost as good as mine." "Almost?" said Susanna. "Not almost. Better."

She tore a thumb-sized piece off one end and popped it into her mouth. And slowly and carefully, she chewed.

That was too much for Huldah.
"All right!" she shouted. "Then tell me, where did you get it?
Who brought the bread?"
"We don't know," said Joanna. "After Jesus finished teaching,
his disciples sorted us into these groups. Then, a little while later,
they passed around the food. But I don't know who brought
the bread. You'll have to ask one of them."

Huldah stomped off.
Sarah, the seamstress, waved at her.
Aaron, the butcher, waved too.
Her cousin Elizabeth called, "Hello!"
But Huldah ignored them all.
She had something more important to do.
Finally, she spotted one of Jesus' disciples
with a huge basket of bread and fish
under his arm.

Huldah grabbed his shoulder
and spun him around.
"I'm sorry," he said.
"Did I miss you?
Or would you like
some more?"

Huldah actually was pretty hungry by now.
And the bread smelled more wonderful than ever.
But she was determined to get an answer.
"Who brought the bread?" Huldah snapped.

"I'm sorry," said the disciple, "but I don't know.
The Master split it up and gave it to us to pass out.
I didn't see where he got it. I suppose you'll have to ask him."
The disciple pointed his finger across the crowd.

So Huldah marched off to find Jesus.
She didn't bother stepping around
the groups, this time.
She plowed straight through them,
like a runaway boulder.
"Huldah!" called a friend,
"Have you tasted the bread?"
"Huldah!" shouted a neighbor,
"it looks like you've got competition."
"Huldah!" hollered her
very own mother,
"you have to get this recipe!"

Huldah looked at the bread in her hand.
The doughy smell hung in the air.
The crusty taste clung to her mouth.

"This bread is delicious," she finally admitted to herself.
"But who could have brought it? And so much of it?
How could anybody bake so many loaves?"

Finally, Huldah marched up to Jesus. His back was turned to her, and he was talking with the crowd.
So she tapped him on the shoulder with one stubby finger.

"Just one question," she interrupted.
"Who brought the bread?"

Jesus turned and smiled, but before he could answer, someone giggled. Someone in the crowd. Someone right behind him.

"Hi, Ma," giggled that someone, again.
It was Nathan, Huldah's youngest son.

"Nathan?" asked Huldah. "What's so funny?
And what are you doing here, anyway? You should be
with the rest of the family."
"Well, I was," said Nathan. "But then it got late,
and everybody got hungry, and one of Jesus' friends —
that man over there — came asking if anybody had any food
to share. "I had that picnic lunch you packed me, remember?
Those five loaves and two fish.

"So I told the man
Jesus could have them.
And Jesus took the fish
and the bread and broke it up
and, somehow, there was enough
for everybody.
"And that's why I was laughing
when you asked who brought the bread.
It looks like you did, Ma!
Well, you and Jesus."

Huldah's face turned oven red.
She felt very foolish. And just a little confused.
"But how?" she said. "How did he make so much?"
"I don't know, Ma," said Nathan.
"Maybe Jesus has a secret recipe too."

Then someone from the crowd called out one more time,
"Great bread, Jesus! Best I ever tasted."
And the woman who brought the bread looked at Jesus
and smiled,
a smile warm and shiny as a fresh-baked bun.